Writing the Dance

Writing the Dance
Workbook & Journal for Dancers

Richard Kent & Josie Bray

Dedications:

For Rylee, my niece—a magical beach dancer and beautiful person… *RK*

For my parents and Kate, who taught me the importance of dance parties in the living room and tangos in the produce aisle … *JB*

Acknowledgments:

Megan Roy, Jenny Carlson Delinks, Erin Pellecchia, Sarah Lovett, Megan Gerlach, Avital Asuleen, Wendy Seyb, Anna Baker-Heans, Megan Flynn, and Rylee Michaud each offered helpful feedback on this book. Sheila Stawinski of the University of Vermont gave us permission to modify and use the Performance Feedback form. Gayle Sirois provided feedback, her editorial eye, and scrumptious peanut butter fudge. Our thanks to all.

NATIONAL WRITING PROJECT

This book is published in cooperation with the National Writing Project, University of California, 2105 Bancroft Way, Berkeley, CA 94720

CONTENTS

"Nobody cares if you can't dance well. Just get up and dance. Great dancers are not great because of their technique, they are great because of their passion."

— Martha Graham

WRITING YOUR DANCE

I have strung ropes from steeple to steeple;
Garlands from window to window;
And golden chains from star to star . . .
And I dance.

—*Arthur Rimbaud*, "Lines"

Keeping a journal is about learning and improving. Scientists and historians, artists and writers all keep journals and notebooks during their research or while working on projects. Even athletes like tennis player Serena Williams and swimming phenom Michael Phelps write to complement their training, competitions, and lives.

Whether you're training at a formal dance school, practicing on your own, or rehearsing for the next big performance, writing in a journal can help you progress as a performer by thinking about and analyzing how you dance. When psychologists work with professional dancers, actors, or athletes, they often have them write reflectively to examine their practice sessions, performances, and personal lives. Such "expressive writing," as it's called, also helps these top-level performers resolve issues of anxiety and fear of failure, while complementing practices like meditation and visualization.

Of course, simply writing about your dance classes, rehearsals, and performances isn't going to replace good teaching or dedicated training. You're not going to instantaneously leap higher or win a leading role because you wrote a journal entry. However, completing the activities in this journal will make you a more knowledgeable dancer. With that knowledge you can improve.

This is your journal. Write what's true for you as a dancer and as a person. Address your weaknesses—don't avoid them—and focus on improvement. Challenge yourself to think deeply, to explore your understanding of dance, and to see yourself at the next level. Allow your writing to broaden what you think is possible. Visualize your best, explore your depth as an artist, and expand your creative capacity.

Why write? Here's what a leading authority of learning and writing says:

> "Writing organizes and clarifies our thoughts. Writing is how we think
> our way into a subject and make it our own. Writing enables us to find
> out what we know—and what we don't know—about whatever we're
> trying to learn." –William Zinsser

Now, turn up the music and dance. Then, pick up your pen, write about it, and learn.

What's in this Workbook & Journal?

At the beginning of each section of the book, you'll find instructions and in some cases a model. Here are the six sections of *Writing the Dance*:

Dance Journals: forty-eight (48) journal prompts to help you think about your dance and yourself. If a particular prompt doesn't work for you, cross it out and write what's uppermost in your mind.

Additional Journal Pages: seven (7) blank pages if you have more to say about a particular journal.

Dance Reflection: sixteen (16) pages that will guide you in analyzing one of your performances or rehearsals.

Performance Feedback: five (5) pages that will help you think about the stressors you face before, during, and after a performance.

Dance Study: eight (8) pages that will guide you in unpacking a performance you watched in person or on video.

Notes Pages: fifteen (15) blank pages to use for notes, drawings, and more.

DANCE JOURNAL PROMPTS

Instructions for Writing Journals

Your journal includes 48 prompts. Many of these prompts can be composed in 3-5 minutes; they're called quick-writes. When you begin a journal entry, try not to stop. Keep your pen or pencil on the paper and keep writing. Quick-writes remind us of improvisational dance, the process of creating movement and being inventive.

If your mind goes blank while you're writing a journal entry, make a list of words related to the topic. When your ideas begin to flow, start writing complete sentences again.

If you run out of space and have more to say, continue writing on the additional blank journal pages provided on pages 59-66. And please don't be overly concerned about the conventions of writing like spelling, grammar, or paragraphing. Just write.

1.

What are your strengths as a dancer right now? When asked to name strengths, some dancers said they were "focused," "dedicated," and "confident." List some of your strengths here:

Now write about your primary strength as a dancer:

2.

Think about an aspect of dance that you'd like to improve upon. Search YouTube to find a video that addresses this dance skill. Watch the video and write about what you observed:

Skill: _____ Title of Video: _____

–What new information did you learn?

–What might you try out or how might you adapt your dancing?

–What questions did you have after watching the video?

–What ideas might you share with a fellow dancer?

–What knowledge might you share with your dance instructor?

–What suggestions, if any, might you make for revising this video?

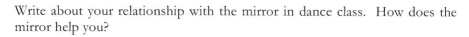

3.

Write about your relationship with the mirror in dance class. How does the mirror help you?

When does the mirror prevent you from doing your best work?

Do you notice any habits you have in front of the mirror that you don't have other places?

Is there anything you'd like to change about your relationship to the mirror? If so, what is the first step you will take toward making that change?

4.

Write about one of your favorite classmates or training partners using the prompts below.

What are this person's qualities as a dancer?

What are this dancer's qualities as a person?

What are this dancer's unique habits or quirks?

Share a story about this dancer:

What have you learned from this person?

What might this dancer have learned from you?

5.

Write about what you do before a performance to give your best on stage.

6.

Who brings out the best in you as a dancer and why? You might first think of a teacher or a dance partner. You could also think about family members, friends, audience members, or classmates.

7.

What makes rehearsal hard for you?

What makes rehearsal easy for you?

8.

My favorite training food is . . .

During a performance I am nervous about . . .

My favorite exercise or activity during rehearsal is . . .

When I hear _____ from a fellow dancer, I feel like . . .

When my dance company, team, or group nails a performance, I feel like...

When my teacher says _____ I feel like...

9.

Tell the story of when you first started dancing.

10.

Outline what you consider a perfect warm-up routine for rehearsal. Make a list of each activity on the left; include the approximate amount of time spent on the activity; and offer a reason you have included it.

Warm-up Activities	How long?	Why this activity?

11.

Write a letter to one of your favorite former teachers. You may wish to include what you're doing now as a dancer, the teacher's contributions to your life, the issues you currently face as a dancer, a fun memory, or a photo. Think about mailing a revised version of the letter to your teacher.

12.

What's the best dance performance that you've seen in person? Describe the details and explain what made it *the best.*

13.

How do you learn dance? Look at this figure and circle the ways you learn as a dancer.

Some of the Ways Dancers Learn

Adapted with permission from *Writing on the Bus (Kent, 2012, p. 14)*

Of the various learning activities above that you did <u>not</u> circle, which ones could you add to your experience to help you improve as a dancer? Explain.

What are the ways you learn technique that are not included in the figure above?

14.

Describe your most humiliating experience as a dancer. What might you have learned from this experience?

15.

In this journal entry, you're going to create a dancer's playlist.

Make a list of your favorite songs down the left side:

Which favorite songs would you play…

The night before a performance:

Song title: _____

During rehearsal:

Song title: _____

The morning of a performance:

Song title: _____

During a sloppy rehearsal:

Song title: _____

After a brilliant performance:

Song title: _____

After a poor performance:

Song title: _____

When a show ends its run:

Song title: _____

Others times: _____
Song title: _____

Others times: _____
Song title: _____

16.

Using your most recent performance, respond to the following:

–Describe the evening before this performance. Did you prepare the way you should have?

–On the day of the performance, how did you spend your time? Did you eat/hydrate adequately? If you could improve one aspect of your preparation for this performance, what would it be?

–Describe your pre-performance (e.g., warm-up). Is there any aspect of your warm-up that you'd improve upon?

–Describe your mindset <u>during</u> a performance. Were you focused and motivated?

–Describe your recovery after a performance. Did you stretch, hydrate, and eat appropriately? Is there any aspect of your post-performance routine that you'd change?

17.

Give an example from your own experience why this statement can be true: "Some days, performing poorly is the most important thing that could happen to a dancer."

18.

Make a list of five qualities you believe an effective dance teacher must have. Write about each quality using a teacher that you know.

Quality _____:

Quality _____:

Quality _____:

Quality _____:

Quality _____:

19.

Think about the roles of dance teacher and choreographer. Perhaps you've done some teaching or choreographing, or maybe not. Whatever your experience, write to the following prompts:

–What are the most challenging aspects of being a dance teacher?

–What are some of the most challenging aspects of being a choreographer?

–As a dancer, is there anything you could do to assist teachers or choreographers with their jobs?

20.

Go outside and dance in a place where people don't usually dance. Write about the experience. How did your body feel to dance outside?

21.

If you could relive one moment as a dancer, what would it be? Why would you want to go back?

22.

Picture a younger dancer that might admire you. How would that dancer describe you as a performer and person?

23.

Select an inspiring piece of artwork that is not dance (e.g., a painting, poem, novel, movie). Imagine that you are going to create a dance inspired by the art. What would the dance look like? How many dancers would there be? What kind of music would you use? Describe your imaginary dance with as much detail as possible. (Remember: You may use the blank pages on p. 59.)

24.

What is something you dislike about yourself as a dancer? Write about how you work on this issue in an effort to improve.

25.

Think back through your dance career. Make a list of five significant experiences you've had at different age levels. What did you learn from each experience? These experiences may include roles you danced, teachers you studied with, new technique you learned, or classmates you enjoyed.

Experience 1. _____:

Experience 2. _____:

Experience 3. _____:

Experience 4. _____:

Experience 5. _____:

26.

How does a good technique class change the way you work in rehearsal? How does a good rehearsal change the way you work in class?

27.

In dance, there are things we can control and things we can't. For example, we can't control our teacher's decisions or what someone says about us. We can control the amount of sleep we get, the volume and quality of training we do, the diet we maintain, and the attitude we bring to a rehearsal or class. Write about a time when you let something you could not control get the better of you. What happened? How did you react? What would you do now under the same circumstances?

28.

Make a list of five good things that are happening in your life right now outside of dance.

1. _____

2. _____

3. _____

4. _____

5. _____

Select one or two and write about them.

29.

It's often said that we are who we spend the most time with. Who are the five people, dancers or not, that you spend the most time with? In what ways do they influence who you are?

30.

Make a list of what you say to yourself during a rehearsal or performance. You may well want to write down this "self-talk" just after a rehearsal or performance. This internal dialog may include feelings, instructions you give yourself, or random thoughts.

31.

Read through your list of self-talk on the previous page and write about what you notice. Is your talk positive, instructive, and motivating? Do you spend too much time complaining about a classmate, teacher, or yourself? In the end, you'll want to decide whether your self-talk is productive or destructive, positive or negative, informative or unhelpful.

32.

Make a list of 10 favorite quotations by dancers, teachers, or choreographers. If you don't already know some, you can do this by looking through dance books or searching online.

33.

Look back at the list of quotations in Journal #32. Choose one or two to write about.

34.

Make a list of people—dancers or not—that you would stand in a very long line to meet. What do these people have in common? In your eyes, what does this list say about you?

35.

Where is your favorite place to dance and why?

36.

Draw your favorite dance pose, position, or step. If you're not much of an artist, stick figures will do.

37.

Have you tried any other sports or physical activities other than dance? If so, in what ways have they helped your dancing?

38.

Watch one of the dance shows on television like *So You Think You Can Dance* or *Dancing with the Stars* and make a list of some the judges' descriptive lines. Write about one of those lines. Choose a line that seemed most accurate to you and write about it. Why do you think the judge said this? How could the dancer best take this feedback in the future? Is there any way that you can use this feedback in your own dancing?

39.

Go somewhere that you can be alone, a private space like your bedroom or a rehearsal room at your dance studio. Put on some music and dance for yourself. Dance to feel good. Do not think about what it looks like. If you are in a studio, turn away from the mirror. Write about this experience.

40.

Go to a dance studio you've never been to before and take a class in a style that you've never studied. What was it like? Describe the experience. How was this new dance form similar to what you've done in the past, and how was it different? How can you use what you learned that day in your regular dance form?

41.

What advice or talk do you <u>least</u> like to hear before a performance? Why?

42.

Come up with four t-shirt slogans/sayings about your ensemble, studio, or dancing. Use the t-shirts provided. To jumpstart your thinking, here is a popular quotation: "And if the music is good, you dance."

43.

Go to YouTube and watch a master dancer's performance. Name the dancer below and list up to sixteen words that describe the dancer's performance. Select one of the words and write about it.

Master Dancer: _____

_____

_____   _____

_____   _____

_____   _____

_____   _____

_____   _____

_____   _____

_____

Your word selection: _____

_____

_____

_____

_____

_____

_____

44.

Draw a picture of your favorite piece of dance clothing or equipment and write one sentence about it.

_____

_____

45.

Select a book or article about a dancer that you've never heard of before. Read some of it and then write about what is interesting to you about this dancer's life? Is there anything about this dancer that reminds you of yourself?

46.

Throughout rehearsals for a show or a dance class season, we all experience highs and lows, ups and down. Think back to a specific time and give quick examples of the following:

I laughed…   I cried or got emotional…

I screamed like a wild person…   I got crazy angry…

I sat and stared in disbelief…   I just didn't care…

I wanted to go hide…   I wanted someone to
                                              see…

47.

We are our thoughts and actions. In the callout bubble below, list the <u>individual</u> words (not phrases or sentences) that you believe represent you as both a dancer and person.

48.

"We write not to say what we know, but to learn, to discover, to know. Writing is thinking, exploring, finding out." –Donald Murray

In what ways has this quotation proven true for you as a dancer who has kept a journal?

ADDITIONAL JOURNAL PAGES

Journal #_____

Journal #_____

Journal #_____

Journal #_____

Journal #_____

Journal #_____

Journal #_____

DANCE REFLECTIONS

Instructions for *Dance Reflections*

The prompts on the following pages provide you with an opportunity to analyze your dancing and will help you improve your understanding of technique, artistry, and, in a real sense, yourself. These prompts can be used for dance class (when you're working on technique), rehearsals (when you're preparing or practicing for a performance), or for a performance itself.

When you fill out a *Dance Reflection*, don't be overly concerned about the conventions of writing. In other words, don't worry about spelling, grammar, and paragraphing... *just write.*

Use the model *Dance Reflection* on the next page to see how a dancer could address certain prompts. But remember, you'll have your own way of telling your dance story.

At the bottom of the sheet, you'll see a quick Dancer Check-in. Don't sit around and ponder life. Give a quick response that reflects your first thought(s). Using this scale to rate each topic:

Above Average (+)   Average (O)   Below Average (–)

As you go through these topics, focus on the following:

Health: How's my over all health?

Sleep: Am I getting enough sleep each night?

Hydration: Do I take in enough water throughout the day as well as
                before, during, and after I dance?

Fitness: How's my overall fitness level?

Nutrition: Have I eaten the suggested foods (i.e., grains, proteins,
                veggies, fruit) for a healthy diet? To learn more you can go to
                the USDA's nutrition website (ChooseMyPlate.Gov).

Now, check out the model on the following pages.

MODEL—Dance Reflection—MODEL

–for class, rehearsal, or a performance–

Dance: *Improv Class*   Place: *Miss Janet's Studio*

Date: *February 16*   Time: *1:00pm – 2:45pm*

- My strengths as a dancer today:

Today I felt my body have an extreme release of tension. I felt comfortable trusting my peers to hold my weight; I feel infinitely less fear now when it comes to worrying about whether or not the movement will be successful or I will fall.

- My weaknesses as a dancer today:

I felt very self-conscious when Miss Janet was watching us during our group improv. While I do usually try to keep my mind on my alignment and make a conscious effort to stay in-tune with my body, I feel like I've been overthinking it. When she's watching, I worry about how I'm doing.

- Our strengths as a duet, trio, or ensemble today:

I LOVED working with Delia. I felt like we formed such a wonderful connection and trust between each other that transcended the friendship we already have. I rolled on top of her back at one point and the push back she gave from her spine not only elevated me off of my feet, but also rotated my contact point, flipping me onto my ribs, and I was floating above the floor for a split second. It felt like defying gravity. It reminded me of going on my favorite roller coaster. It was exhilarating.

- Our weaknesses as a duet, trio, or ensemble today:

We were so into our duet that I stopped paying attention to the other dancers in the room and accidentally bumped into Adam! He wasn't hurt, but it taught me that I need to pay more attention.

- Whose performance did you most admire today and why?

Susannah and Matt's duet was beautiful. They seemed so connected and as though the movement just flowed out of them. It looked like it was choreographed! They performed with grace and energy and were such a joy to watch.

- Other comments (e.g., working as a company or ensemble, attitude, preparation, supporting other dancers....)

During the performance pieces, I felt more in-tune with the group and felt like we were all more committed as a whole. Having the option to break from contact really expanded the possibilities of impulses we could delve into, which led to more playful and personally beneficial group work than I'd felt thus far. I can feel us all becoming better performers from improv.

Dancer Check-in

Above Average (+)   Average (O)   Below Average (–)

Health: O	*Nutrition:* Grains: O
Sleep: –	Protein: –
Hydration: +	Veggies: –
Fitness: O	Fruit: +

Life Beyond Dance: O

I'm really tired. I should probably try to sleep more, but it's really hard to find time between rehearsal, class, and homework. I hope it will get easier once I turn in my English paper on Friday.

Notes and Scribbles:

Quote of the day from Erin!

"I'm CRAZZZZZZZZZIIIIIEEEE!"

LOL!

Dance Reflection

—for class, rehearsal, or a performance—

Dance: _____   Place:_____

Date:_____   Time:_____

-   My strengths as a dancer today:

-   My weaknesses as a dancer today:

-   Our strengths as a duet, trio, or ensemble today:

-   Our weaknesses as a duet, trio, or ensemble today:

-   Whose performance did you most admire today and why?

- Other comments (e.g., working as a company or ensemble, attitude, preparation, supporting other dancers....)

Dancer Check-in

Above Average (+)   Average (O)   Below Average (–)

Health: *Nutrition:* Grains:

Sleep: Protein:

Hydration: Veggies:

Fitness: Fruit:

Life Beyond Dance:

Notes and Scribbles:

Dance Reflection

—for class, rehearsal, or a performance—

Dance: _____   Place:_____

Date: _____   Time:_____

- My strengths as a dancer today:

- My weaknesses as a dancer today:

- Our strengths as a duet, trio, or ensemble today:

- Our weaknesses as a duet, trio, or ensemble today:

- Whose performance did you most admire today and why?

- Other comments (e.g., working as a company or ensemble, attitude, preparation, supporting other dancers….)

Dancer Check-in

Above Average (+)   Average (O)   Below Average (–)

Health: *Nutrition:* Grains:

Sleep: Protein:

Hydration: Veggies:

Fitness: Fruit:

Life Beyond Dance:

Notes and Scribbles:

Dance Reflection

—for class, rehearsal, or a performance—

Dance: _____   Place:_____

Date: _____   Time:_____

- My strengths as a dancer today:

- My weaknesses as a dancer today:

- Our strengths as a duet, trio, or ensemble today:

- Our weaknesses as a duet, trio, or ensemble today:

- Whose performance did you most admire today and why?

– Other comments (e.g., working as a company or ensemble, attitude, preparation, supporting other dancers….)

Dancer Check-in

Above Average (+)   Average (O)   Below Average (–)

Health: *Nutrition:* Grains:

Sleep: Protein:

Hydration: Veggies:

Fitness: Fruit:

Life Beyond Dance:

Notes and Scribbles:

Dance Reflection

—for class, rehearsal, or a performance—

Dance: _____   Place:_____

Date:_____   Time:_____

- My strengths as a dancer today:

- My weaknesses as a dancer today:

- Our strengths as a duet, trio, or ensemble today:

- Our weaknesses as a duet, trio, or ensemble today:

- Whose performance did you most admire today and why?

- Other comments (e.g., working as a company or ensemble, attitude, preparation, supporting other dancers....)

Dancer Check-in

Above Average (+)   Average (O)   Below Average (–)

Health: *Nutrition:* Grains:

Sleep: Protein:

Hydration: Veggies:

Fitness: Fruit:

Life Beyond Dance:

Notes and Scribbles:

Dance Reflection

—for class, rehearsal, or a performance—

Dance: _____   Place:_____

Date:_____   Time:_____

- My strengths as a dancer today:

- My weaknesses as a dancer today:

- Our strengths as a duet, trio, or ensemble today:

- Our weaknesses as a duet, trio, or ensemble today:

- Whose performance did you most admire today and why?

–   Other comments (e.g., working as a company or ensemble, attitude, preparation, supporting other dancers....)

Dancer Check-in

Above Average (+)   Average (O)   Below Average (–)

Health: *Nutrition:* Grains:

Sleep: Protein:

Hydration: Veggies:

Fitness: Fruit:

Life Beyond Dance:

Notes and Scribbles:

Dance Reflection

—for class, rehearsal, or a performance—

Dance: _____   Place:_____

Date:_____   Time:_____

– My strengths as a dancer today:

– My weaknesses as a dancer today:

– Our strengths as a duet, trio, or ensemble today:

– Our weaknesses as a duet, trio, or ensemble today:

– Whose performance did you most admire today and why?

—   Other comments (e.g., working as a company or ensemble, attitude, preparation, supporting other dancers….)

Dancer Check-in

Above Average (+)   Average (O)   Below Average (–)

Health: *Nutrition:* Grains:

Sleep: Protein:

Hydration: Veggies:

Fitness: Fruit:

Life Beyond Dance:

Notes and Scribbles:

Dance Reflection
—for class, rehearsal, or a performance—

Dance: _____   Place:_____

Date:_____   Time:_____

- My strengths as a dancer today:

- My weaknesses as a dancer today:

- Our strengths as a duet, trio, or ensemble today:

- Our weaknesses as a duet, trio, or ensemble today:

- Whose performance did you most admire today and why?

- Other comments (e.g., working as a company or ensemble, attitude, preparation, supporting other dancers....)

Dancer Check-in

Above Average (+)   Average (O)   Below Average (–)

Health: *Nutrition:* Grains:

Sleep: Protein:

Hydration: Veggies:

Fitness: Fruit:

Life Beyond Dance:

Notes and Scribbles:

Dance Reflection

—for class, rehearsal, or a performance—

Dance: _____   Place:_____

Date:_____   Time:_____

- My strengths as a dancer today:

- My weaknesses as a dancer today:

- Our strengths as a duet, trio, or ensemble today:

- Our weaknesses as a duet, trio, or ensemble today:

- Whose performance did you most admire today and why?

–   Other comments (e.g., working as a company or ensemble, attitude, preparation, supporting other dancers….)

Dancer Check-in

Above Average (+)   Average (O)   Below Average (–)

Health: *Nutrition:* Grains:

Sleep: Protein:

Hydration: Veggies:

Fitness: Fruit:

Life Beyond Dance:

Notes and Scribbles:

Dance Reflection
—for class, rehearsal, or a performance—

Dance: _____   Place:_____

Date:_____   Time:_____

- My strengths as a dancer today:

- My weaknesses as a dancer today:

- Our strengths as a duet, trio, or ensemble today:

- Our weaknesses as a duet, trio, or ensemble today:

- Whose performance did you most admire today and why?

–   Other comments (e.g., working as a company or ensemble, attitude, preparation, supporting other dancers….)

Dancer Check-in

Above Average (+)   Average (O)   Below Average (–)

Health: *Nutrition:* Grains:

Sleep: Protein:

Hydration: Veggies:

Fitness: Fruit:

Life Beyond Dance:

Notes and Scribbles:

Dance Reflection

—for class, rehearsal, or a performance—

Dance: _____   Place:_____

Date:_____   Time:_____

-   My strengths as a dancer today:

-   My weaknesses as a dancer today:

-   Our strengths as a duet, trio, or ensemble today:

-   Our weaknesses as a duet, trio, or ensemble today:

-   Whose performance did you most admire today and why?

– Other comments (e.g., working as a company or ensemble, attitude, preparation, supporting other dancers....)

Dancer Check-in

Above Average (+) Average (O) Below Average (–)

Health: *Nutrition:* Grains:

Sleep: Protein:

Hydration: Veggies:

Fitness: Fruit:

Life Beyond Dance:

Notes and Scribbles:

Dance Reflection

—for class, rehearsal, or a performance—

Dance: _____   Place:_____

Date:_____   Time:_____

- My strengths as a dancer today:

- My weaknesses as a dancer today:

- Our strengths as a duet, trio, or ensemble today:

- Our weaknesses as a duet, trio, or ensemble today:

- Whose performance did you most admire today and why?

– Other comments (e.g., working as a company or ensemble, attitude, preparation, supporting other dancers….)

Dancer Check-in

Above Average (+)   Average (O)   Below Average (–)

Health: *Nutrition:* Grains:

Sleep: Protein:

Hydration: Veggies:

Fitness: Fruit:

Life Beyond Dance:

Notes and Scribbles:

Dance Reflection

—for class, rehearsal, or a performance—

Dance: _____   Place:_____

Date:_____   Time:_____

- My strengths as a dancer today:

- My weaknesses as a dancer today:

- Our strengths as a duet, trio, or ensemble today:

- Our weaknesses as a duet, trio, or ensemble today:

- Whose performance did you most admire today and why?

– Other comments (e.g., working as a company or ensemble, attitude, preparation, supporting other dancers….)

Dancer Check-in

Above Average (+)   Average (O)   Below Average (–)

Health: *Nutrition:* Grains:

Sleep: Protein:

Hydration: Veggies:

Fitness: Fruit:

Life Beyond Dance:

Notes and Scribbles:

Dance Reflection

—for class, rehearsal, or a performance—

Dance: _____   Place:_____

Date:_____   Time:_____

- My strengths as a dancer today:

- My weaknesses as a dancer today:

- Our strengths as a duet, trio, or ensemble today:

- Our weaknesses as a duet, trio, or ensemble today:

- Whose performance did you most admire today and why?

– Other comments (e.g., working as a company or ensemble, attitude, preparation, supporting other dancers....)

Dancer Check-in

Above Average (+)   Average (O)   Below Average (–)

Health: *Nutrition:* Grains:

Sleep: Protein:

Hydration: Veggies:

Fitness: Fruit:

Life Beyond Dance:

Notes and Scribbles:

Dance Reflection

—for class, rehearsal, or a performance—

Dance: _____   Place:_____

Date:_____   Time:_____

- My strengths as a dancer today:

- My weaknesses as a dancer today:

- Our strengths as a duet, trio, or ensemble today:

- Our weaknesses as a duet, trio, or ensemble today:

- Whose performance did you most admire today and why?

– Other comments (e.g., working as a company or ensemble, attitude, preparation, supporting other dancers....)

Dancer Check-in

Above Average (+)   Average (O)   Below Average (–)

Health: *Nutrition:* Grains:

Sleep: Protein:

Hydration: Veggies:

Fitness: Fruit:

Life Beyond Dance:

Notes and Scribbles:

Dance Reflection

—for class, rehearsal, or a performance—

Dance: _____   Place:_____

Date:_____   Time:_____

- My strengths as a dancer today:

- My weaknesses as a dancer today:

- Our strengths as a duet, trio, or ensemble today:

- Our weaknesses as a duet, trio, or ensemble today:

- Whose performance did you most admire today and why?

– Other comments (e.g., working as a company or ensemble, attitude, preparation, supporting other dancers….)

Dancer Check-in

Above Average (+)   Average (O)   Below Average (–)

Health: *Nutrition:* Grains:

Sleep: Protein:

Hydration: Veggies:

Fitness: Fruit:

Life Beyond Dance:

Notes and Scribbles:

Dance Reflection

—for class, rehearsal, or a performance—

Dance: _____   Place:_____

Date:_____   Time:_____

- My strengths as a dancer today:

- My weaknesses as a dancer today:

- Our strengths as a duet, trio, or ensemble today:

- Our weaknesses as a duet, trio, or ensemble today:

- Whose performance did you most admire today and why?

– Other comments (e.g., working as a company or ensemble, attitude, preparation, supporting other dancers….)

Dancer Check-in

Above Average (+)   Average (O)   Below Average (–)

Health: *Nutrition:* Grains:

Sleep: Protein:

Hydration: Veggies:

Fitness: Fruit:

Life Beyond Dance:

Notes and Scribbles:

PERFORMANCE FEEDBACK

Instructions for Performance Feedback

At different times fill out one of the following Performance Feedback forms immediately after a performance. This writing will help you look closely at the stress you experience before and during a performance. As a dancer, writing about stressors can help you manage those feelings in the future.

—MODEL—

Performance Feedback

PERFORMANCE: *Nutcracker #4*   **DATE:** *December 1*

What stressors did you experience before, during, and after this performance?

I was nervous today before and during the show because it was the first time my friends came to the show. Amy and Claire were there today. After the show, I wasn't sure if they liked it or not since they've never seen Ballet before.

How did you experience this stress? Did it manifest in your thoughts, in the way you felt, or in the way you acted?

Leading up to the show I couldn't stop talking because I was so excited and nervous. My stomach had butterflies, too. During Act 1, I was okay, but then during intermission I had a chance to think about it again and got nervous for my solo in Act II. During my solo I was thinking about Claire and Amy more than dancing, and I fell off pointe during my pirouettes. I was so mad and disappointed that I messed up in front of them!

Mark on this scale your level of excitement and motivation for the match.

0-------------------------------------5-----------------/---------------------10
      Too Low   Perfect   Too High

In a few words, describe your feelings at the various times in the day?

  Travel to performance: *nervous, jittery*
  Warm up: *excited, happy*
  Just before the performance: *scared!*
  During the performance: *Better, then scared again, then disappointed*
  After the performance: *a little anxious but then relieved*

What techniques did you use to manage any stress you experienced? How effective were you in controlling this stress?

Molly showed me how to breathe to calm down backstage and that helped me a little bit. I was okay until act II. I was upset when I fell off pointe and wasn't very good at controlling stress right then. After my solo I went off stage and saw Molly again. She helped me calm down, and when I came back on stage for the finale I was more relaxed.

How was your self-talk? Positive, negative, thoughtful?

It was negative after I fell out of the turns, but when I went off stage, Molly helped me get back into the show. When I went back out I was determined not to mess up. That was when I was positive and I told myself I could do it.

Describe how your stressors, excitement/motivation, and self-talk impacted your performance.

I don't usually fall out of pirouettes, so I really think that was because I psyched myself up for Claire and Amy. I don't think I've ever been that nervous before. Talking with Molly backstage helped me calm down so I wouldn't mess up again.

After unpacking your performance-day mental state, what would you do differently to improve for the next performance?

Next time I have friends coming to see me dance, I won't talk to them before curtain. It just made me too nervous and I couldn't concentrate. Instead of talking so much before the show I will be quiet and take time to myself to warm up and get into the zone.

What's one thing you learned from completing this Performance Feedback form?

I was so lucky to have an older dancer like Molly backstage to help me out when I messed up and was scared!

Performance Feedback

Performance: _____ Date: _____

What stressors did you experience before, during and after this performance?

How did you experience this stress? Did it manifest in your thoughts, in the way you felt, or in the way you acted?

Mark on this scale your level of excitement/motivation for the performance.

0------------------------------------5------------------------------------10

Too Low   Perfect   Too High

In a few words, describe your feelings at the various times in the day?

Travel to performance:

Warm up:

Just before the performance:

During the performance:

After the performance:

What techniques did you use to manage any stress you experienced? How effective were you in controlling this stress?

How was your self-talk? Positive, negative, thoughtful?

Describe how your stressors, excitement/motivation, and self-talk impacted your performance.

After unpacking your performance-day mental state, what would you do differently to improve for the next performance?

What's one thing you learned from completing this Performance Feedback form?

Performance Feedback

Performance: _____ Date: _____

What stressors did you experience before, during and after this performance?

How did you experience this stress? Did it manifest in your thoughts, in the way you felt, or in the way you acted?

Mark on this scale your level of excitement/motivation for the performance.

0--5--10

      Too Low   Perfect   Too High

In a few words, describe your feelings at the various times in the day?

      Travel to performance:

      Warm up:

      Just before the performance:

      During the performance:

      After the performance:

What techniques did you use to manage any stress you experienced? How effective were you in controlling this stress?

How was your self-talk? Positive, negative, thoughtful?

Describe how your stressors, excitement/motivation, and self-talk impacted your performance.

After unpacking your performance-day mental state, what would you do differently to improve for the next performance?

What's one thing you learned from completing this Performance Feedback form?

Performance Feedback

Performance: _____ Date: _____

What stressors did you experience before, during and after this performance?

How did you experience this stress? Did it manifest in your thoughts, in the way you felt, or in the way you acted?

Mark on this scale your level of excitement/motivation for the performance.

0--5--10

      Too Low   Perfect   Too High

In a few words, describe your feelings at the various times in the day?

Travel to performance:

Warm up:

Just before the performance:

During the performance:

After the performance:

What techniques did you use to manage any stress you experienced? How effective were you in controlling this stress?

How was your self-talk? Positive, negative, thoughtful?

Describe how your stressors, excitement/motivation, and self-talk impacted your performance.

After unpacking your performance-day mental state, what would you do differently to improve for the next performance?

What's one thing you learned from completing this Performance Feedback form?

Performance Feedback

Performance: _____ Date: _____

What stressors did you experience before, during and after this performance?

How did you experience this stress? Did it manifest in your thoughts, in the way you felt, or in the way you acted?

Mark on this scale your level of excitement/motivation for the performance.

0--5--10

    Too Low   Perfect   Too High

In a few words, describe your feelings at the various times in the day?

Travel to performance:

Warm up:

Just before the performance:

During the performance:

After the performance:

What techniques did you use to manage any stress you experienced? How effective were you in controlling this stress?

How was your self-talk? Positive, negative, thoughtful?

Describe how your stressors, excitement/motivation, and self-talk impacted your performance.

After unpacking your performance-day mental state, what would you do differently to improve for the next performance?

What's one thing you learned from completing this Performance Feedback form?

Performance Feedback

Performance: _____ Date: _____

What stressors did you experience before, during and after this performance?

How did you experience this stress? Did it manifest in your thoughts, in the way you felt, or in the way you acted?

Mark on this scale your level of excitement/motivation for the performance.

0------------------------------------5------------------------------------10

      Too Low   Perfect   Too High

In a few words, describe your feelings at the various times in the day?

    Travel to performance:

    Warm up:

    Just before the performance:

    During the performance:

    After the performance:

What techniques did you use to manage any stress you experienced? How effective were you in controlling this stress?

How was your self-talk? Positive, negative, thoughtful?

Describe how your stressors, excitement/motivation, and self-talk impacted your performance.

After unpacking your performance-day mental state, what would you do differently to improve for the next performance?

What's one thing you learned from completing this Performance Feedback form?

DANCE STUDIES

Instructions for Dance Studies

It's time to go to the theatre! Go to a live dance performance. After the performance, use these questions to reflect and think critically on what you have seen. Notice that you will be asked to pay particular attention to one dancer in the performance.

This reflection is a learning activity that will challenge you to watch a performance more critically, more fully, and more like a teacher than a performer.

Dance Study pages could also be used for watching video performances or rehearsals at your studio or someone else's.

Dance Study

Performance _____ Date_____

Selected Dancer _____

Think about the dancer you selected to watch. What were this dancer's strengths? Weaknesses? That special *something*?

Give some examples of when your dancer seemed most emotionally connected to the work.

Think about the entire performance. What was the overall feeling, energy, or mood of the dance? Did this performance remind you of any you've seen before? If so, write about them.

Describe the story or meaning this dance may have attempted to communicate to the audience.

Did the choreography of the dance showcase the dancers' strengths? Give examples in your explanation.

In what ways did the design elements of the performance (e.g., costumes, scenery, lighting) contribute to the dance? Did these elements ever distract or take away from the movement? Explain.

What was your favorite image or stage picture from the dance? Draw that moment as you remember it:

Which pieces of choreography were the most interesting to you? Try to do some of that choreography yourself. Write about your experience.

What's your overall takeaway from watching this dance?

Notes

Dance Study

Performance _____ Date_____

Selected Dancer _____

Think about the dancer you selected to watch. What were this dancer's strengths? Weaknesses? That special *something*?

Give some examples of when your dancer seemed most emotionally connected to the work.

Think about the entire performance. What was the overall feeling, energy, or mood of the dance? Did this performance remind you of any you've seen before? If so, write about them.

Describe the story or meaning this dance may have attempted to communicate to the audience.

Did the choreography of the dance showcase the dancers' strengths? Give examples in your explanation.

In what ways did the design elements of the performance (e.g., costumes, scenery, lighting) contribute to the dance? Did these elements ever distract or take away from the movement? Explain.

What was your favorite image or stage picture from the dance? Draw that moment as you remember it:

Which pieces of choreography were the most interesting to you? Try to do some of that choreography yourself. Write about your experience.

What's your overall takeaway from watching this dance?

Notes

Dance Study

Performance _____ Date_____

Selected Dancer _____

Think about the dancer you selected to watch. What were this dancer's strengths? Weaknesses? That special *something*?

Give some examples of when your dancer seemed most emotionally connected to the work.

Think about the entire performance. What was the overall feeling, energy, or mood of the dance? Did this performance remind you of any you've seen before? If so, write about them.

Describe the story or meaning this dance may have attempted to communicate to the audience.

Did the choreography of the dance showcase the dancers' strengths? Give examples in your explanation.

In what ways did the design elements of the performance (e.g., costumes, scenery, lighting) contribute to the dance? Did these elements ever distract or take away from the movement? Explain.

What was your favorite image or stage picture from the dance? Draw that moment as you remember it:

Which pieces of choreography were the most interesting to you? Try to do some of that choreography yourself. Write about your experience.

What's your overall takeaway from watching this dance?

Notes

Dance Study

Performance _____ Date_____

Selected Dancer _____

Think about the dancer you selected to watch. What were this dancer's strengths? Weaknesses? That special *something*?

Give some examples of when your dancer seemed most emotionally connected to the work.

Think about the entire performance. What was the overall feeling, energy, or mood of the dance? Did this performance remind you of any you've seen before? If so, write about them.

Describe the story or meaning this dance may have attempted to communicate to the audience.

Did the choreography of the dance showcase the dancers' strengths? Give examples in your explanation.

In what ways did the design elements of the performance (e.g., costumes, scenery, lighting) contribute to the dance? Did these elements ever distract or take away from the movement? Explain.

What was your favorite image or stage picture from the dance? Draw that moment as you remember it:

Which pieces of choreography were the most interesting to you? Try to do some of that choreography yourself. Write about your experience.

What's your overall takeaway from watching this dance?

Notes

Dance Study

Performance _____ Date_____

Selected Dancer _____

Think about the dancer you selected to watch. What were this dancer's strengths? Weaknesses? That special *something*?

Give some examples of when your dancer seemed most emotionally connected to the work.

Think about the entire performance. What was the overall feeling, energy, or mood of the dance? Did this performance remind you of any you've seen before? If so, write about them.

Describe the story or meaning this dance may have attempted to communicate to the audience.

Did the choreography of the dance showcase the dancers' strengths? Give examples in your explanation.

In what ways did the design elements of the performance (e.g., costumes, scenery, lighting) contribute to the dance? Did these elements ever distract or take away from the movement? Explain.

What was your favorite image or stage picture from the dance? Draw that
moment as you remember it:

Which pieces of choreography were the most interesting to you? Try to do some of that choreography yourself. Write about your experience.

What's your overall takeaway from watching this dance?

Notes

Dance Study

Performance _____ Date_____

Selected Dancer _____

Think about the dancer you selected to watch. What were this dancer's strengths? Weaknesses? That special *something*?

Give some examples of when your dancer seemed most emotionally connected to the work.

Think about the entire performance. What was the overall feeling, energy, or mood of the dance? Did this performance remind you of any you've seen before? If so, write about them.

Describe the story or meaning this dance may have attempted to communicate to the audience.

Did the choreography of the dance showcase the dancers' strengths? Give examples in your explanation.

In what ways did the design elements of the performance (e.g., costumes, scenery, lighting) contribute to the dance? Did these elements ever distract or take away from the movement? Explain.

What was your favorite image or stage picture from the dance? Draw that moment as you remember it:

Which pieces of choreography were the most interesting to you? Try to do some of that choreography yourself. Write about your experience.

What's your overall takeaway from watching this dance?

Notes

NOTES PAGES

DATE_____   TITLE_____

NOTES

DATE_____   TITLE_____

NOTES

DATE_____   TITLE_____

NOTES

DATE_____   TITLE_____

NOTES

DATE_____   TITLE_____

NOTES

DATE_____   TITLE_____

NOTES

DATE_____   TITLE_____

NOTES

DATE_____   TITLE_____

NOTES

DATE_____   TITLE_____

NOTES

DATE_____   TITLE_____

NOTES

DATE_____   TITLE_____

NOTES

DATE_____   TITLE_____

NOTES

DATE_____   TITLE_____

NOTES

DATE_____   TITLE_____

NOTES

DATE_____   TITLE_____

NOTES

ABOUT THE AUTHORS

Richard Kent

Josie Bray

Richard Kent is a professor at the University of Maine. He is also the co-director of the Maine Writing Project, a site of the National Writing Project. The award-winning author of many books, including *Writing on the Bus*, *The Athlete's Workbook*, and *Room 109,* Kent works with teachers, students, athletes, and coaches at all levels. In his free time, he can be found running, hiking, or cross-country skiing the western mountains of Maine with his Bernese Mountain Dog, Bailey Tuckerman. He maintains a resource website at WritingAthletes.com

Josie Bray is a director-choreographer who has worked at regional and Off-Broadway theatres, and as an assistant on several national tours and the recent Broadway Revival of *Ragtime.* Josie was the Co-Artistic director of the Animus Ensemble, a Boston-based theatre company, for five years and also served as the Executive Director of Green Street Studios, Center for Movement and Dance. She currently teaches at Emerson College and is producing a new musical intended for Broadway. Josie practices yoga and Pilates, experiments in the kitchen, and spends time with her hilarious husband, Jack, and their energetic preschooler, Redd.

Write. Learn. Perform.